The Concise Guide to
D.I.Y.

igloobooks

Published in 2014
by Igloo Books Ltd
Cottage Farm
Sywell
NN6 0BJ
www.igloobooks.com

All content and images
supplied courtesy of Janice Anderssen, Home-Dzine

HUN001 0214
2 4 6 8 10 9 7 5 3 1
ISBN 978-1-78197-071-3

Printed and manufactured in China

The Concise Guide to

D.I.Y.

CONTENTS

INTRODUCTION

DIY – for some people a troublesome task and for others a rewarding and enjoyable hobby. Whichever description suits you best there will be something inside this book for you.

Every home has its problems from time to time. A cupboard that won't close in the kitchen. Blinds in the bedroom that won't fit properly. A doorknob that keeps falling off. Or sometimes you may develop more serious problems such as damp or a leaky roof. It's important to know what tools to get and what to do first if you want to avoid hiring expensive workmen for each and every task.

The chapters in this book focus either on separate types of task, or different rooms of the house to make finding solutions to your problems quick and easy. For each DIY problem there is a step-by-step guide to putting things right and achieving a satisfactory solution.

More advanced DIY-ers can also take advantage of the pages on woodworking tasks, using more advanced tools such as jigsaws and circular saws. For the really adventurous or experienced, have a go at some outdoor jobs such as mending a leaky roof or fixing broken tiles.

There are even ideas for 'projects' that anyone can try, such as spray painting furniture to give your home a new look.

Whatever your DIY level, whether a reluctant fixer-upper or a DIY weekend enthusiast, this book is a useful reference guide for you and your home. Keep it handy!

TOOLS
AND TOOL
MAINTENANCE

HOW TO USE A SPIRIT LEVEL

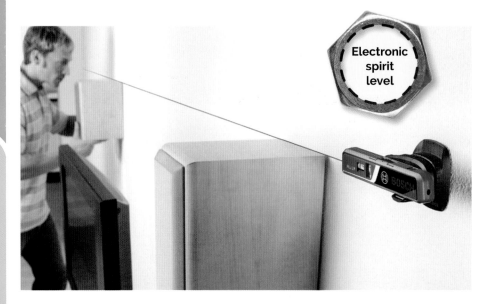

Electronic spirit level

No DIYer should ever be without a spirit level – small or large. A spirit level is used for determining horizontal and vertical levels.

A spirit level indicates whether a surface is level on the horizontal or vertical planes. The most important feature on any spirit level is the glass or plastic vial. This vial contains a coloured liquid that has a bubble of air that moves horizontally or vertically along the vial.

Manual spirit level

STABILA®
MADE IN GERMANY

POCKET BASIC

Colourants tend to be added to the liquid to make it easier to see the bubble. Alcohols are often used in spirit levels because they have a wider range of liquid temperature than water, so there is less chance of the vial breaking owing to ice expansion.

To use a spirit level properly the level should be positioned in the centre, on a firm horizontal or vertical surface. If the plane to be checked is not even, place a straightedge on top and the spirit level on top of the straightedge.

The bubble should sit between the graduation marks. Where the bubble sits over or out of the graduation marks, adjust the left or right side.

When you need to check vertical levels, place the back edge of the spirit level against a straightedge, which you should then position against the vertical plane to check it.

If the bubble is between the graduations, the plane is level. Where the bubble lies outside the graduations, move the straightedge until the bubble is centrally placed. This will allow you to determine any unevenness on the vertical plane.

The best spirit level to buy is one that features both a horizontal and vertical vial. The vials feature two graduation marks that are spaced to allow positioning of the bubble between them. The position of the bubble then indicates whether the horizontal or vertical plane is level.

USING A SCREWDRIVER BIT

One common problem is using a cordless screwdriver or drill/driver. It is important to use the right screwdriver bit for the type of screw being used. As a general guide, if the screw stays on the bit and doesn't fall off, you are using the right bit.

Always make sure that the screwdriver bit is firmly seated in the screw head. As you are drilling, apply pressure to the top of the screwdriver or drill/driver to ensure the bit stays in the screw head as you drill. To prevent the bit or screw slipping as you drive into the wood, gently grip the sides of the screw to hold it in place until it starts to bite into the wood. This is fine for pine, but if you are driving into material such as hardwood, pre-drill a pilot hole.

If you find that the screwdriver bit still slips out of the screw head, you are not applying enough pressure to keep it firmly seated in the head. Compensate by pushing down harder with your left hand on top of the back end of the drill, or by putting your shoulder into it.

Remember to ease back on the pressure when the screw is almost in place. Too much pressure and you will end up sinking the screw too deeply into the wood or board. Quick bursts on and off will also give you more control over how deep the screw is driven into the timber or board.

As they say, practice makes perfect, and the more you drive in screws - the more you know what works best for you.

TIPS

Use a magnetic holder for your screwdriver bits. This will also hold the screw in place on the end of the bit. Where you are placing the screw, push down hard to make an indent and this will make holding the screw straight easier.

NOTES

- -

- -

- -

- -

- -

- -

- -

- -

- -

- -

- -

- -

USING A JIGSAW

Jigsaws are the perfect power tool for cutting curves and complex shapes. Once you become more confident, you will discover many ways to use it for projects around the home.

A jigsaw is also the perfect tool for cutting short, straight lengths of softwoods up to a thickness of 68mm. There are so many ways to use it.

Wood veneers

Most wood-cutting blades for jigsaws are designed so the teeth cut on the upstroke. For fine work demanding less chipping – in wood veneers, for example – an alternative is to place masking tape on the cutting line path before drawing on the pattern line. Another option is to score the veneer along the cutting line with an appropriate craft knife.

Cutting curves

Begin by pressing the base plate firmly on the piece with the blade away from the edge. Switch on and guide the blade along the outside of the cutting line, moving from the start of the curve to the inside corner. Don't apply too much pressure and ensure that the blade stays vertical. Always use a sharp blade and avoid forcing the saw through the cut.

Straight cuts

Hold the piece firmly and guide the saw steadily against a saw fence. Avoid driving blades into the bench top (bending and breaking them) by using rails to raise the piece.

Cut-outs in laminate worktops

If you need to do cut-outs, to insert a kitchen sink, for example, drill a starter hole 10 or 12mm in diameter that allows insertion of the jigsaw blade, and follow the cutting line drawn on masking tape. Avoid scratches by affixing masking tape to the bottom of the base plate.

Mitre cuts

The base plate can be swivelled by 45 degrees to the left or right for mitre cuts. Remove the saw blade and loosen the screw in the base plate; slide the base plate towards the cable end. The base plate has adjustment notches on the left and right at 0, 22.5 and 45 degrees. Swivel the base plate to the desired position.

Choosing the right blade

The key to excellent results with a jigsaw is to match a specific blade to the type of material you will be cutting: wood, metal, plastics or other materials. Always check the package labelling when buying blades.

Photo frame project - a pictorial guide.

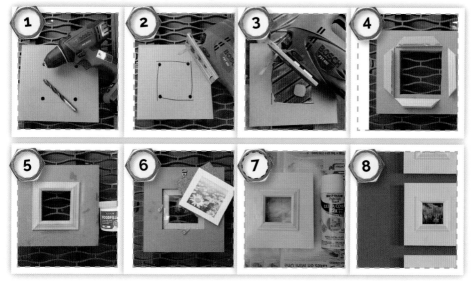

USING A CIRCULAR SAW

A hand-held circular saw is one of the tools that every DIY enthusiast should have. It cuts any kind of timber and board quickly and accurately.

Remember that this is a deceptively dangerous power tool and needs to be handled with care and safety.

Because a circular saw is compact, relatively lightweight, and its blade is nearly always covered by either the guard or the wood you are cutting, it's easy to become careless when using it. Make sure you understand the safety instructions that come with the tool, and follow them carefully whenever you are working.

What is a rip cut?

A rip cut is rough cut, generally used to cut large sections down to size by cutting in the same direction as the wood grain.

What is a cross cut?

A cross cut is also used to trim large sections down to size, but across the grain of the wood.

TIPS

1. Always use the correct blade for the material you will be cutting and ensure that it is properly seated and tightened. Never use dull blades as they will bind to the wood and overheat.

2. Ensure that the wood is sufficiently supported on both sides and ends and clamp smaller pieces if you have to.

3. Check for knots or nails before cutting any piece.

4. When operating a circular saw, start the blade before it meets the wood. Be comfortable when holding the unit – don't over-reach. Don't push the saw, simply guide the unit along the cutting line.

5. Electrical cables and cords should be positioned safely out of the way. Be prepared for a lot of mess, and if you are not using a vacuum hose connection, stand clear of the outlet.

What is a Plunge Cut?

A plunge cut is done when the blade cannot start at the edge of the board, such as when cutting a hole in kitchen countertops or floors. To make this cut, place the front of the shoe against the piece. Then, turn on the saw and slowly lower the blade into the material.

NOTES

- -

- -

- -

- -

- -

- -

- -

- -

USING AN ELECTRIC PLANER

Using an electric planer allows you to shave, trim and easily remove excess wood for edges. You can use this for cutting doors to size, levelling uneven floorboards or planks and removing saw roughness.

Read the instruction manual thoroughly before use.

To change the blade on your planer you will need to use the allen key that is supplied with the planer. Use the allen key to loosen the blade plate located underneath the machine on the drum.

Most planers have two cutting edges, so you simply need to remove the dull blade, turn it over, and re-insert it before tightening it up.

1. Wear safety glasses to ensure you are protected from wood shavings.

2. Unless you are levelling an uneven cut, always start the planer with the front of the machine at a straight level on the wood and the cutting blade away from the edge of the wood.

3. Gently guide the planer onto the wood and across the surface.

After a few practice runs you will soon get the hang of balancing pressure on the front knob. Don't push too hard, simply guide the planer along and let it cut at its own pace to avoid blunting the cutting blade. Stop when the blade has passed the edge and hold the planer firmly to prevent dipping at the edge of the project. After cutting, rest the planer on its side until the blade stops spinning.

4. For smaller projects, securely clamp the piece before using a planer.

5. Use a planer to chamfer (cut corners at a 45-degree angle), adjusting the cutting depth as required. Continue making long, smooth passes until you reach the desired depth.

6. To level uneven sections, mark the uneven areas with a pencil mark and use this as a guide to shave off small amounts at a time.

Always clean the planer after use. Brush to clean off dust and wipe the base plate.

USE THE RIGHT SANDER

There are various sanders available. For large-scale projects, an electric sander can be an extremely useful, time-saving tool. For smaller jobs, a hand-held or cordless version is sufficient.

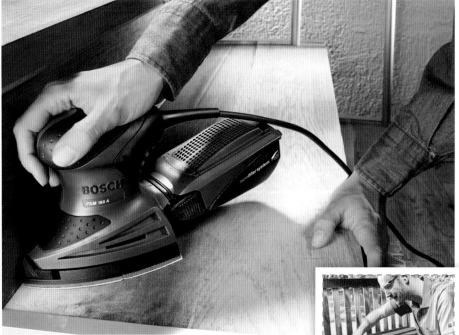

Multi sander

Ideal for a beginner, a multi sander fits comfortably into your hand and can be used for all types of sanding. It is especially effective in furniture restoration projects as its triangular sanding plate can get into any corners.

Cordless multi sander

Use the cordless multi sander anywhere and you don't have to worry about power. The long-lasting lithium-ion battery is always ready when you need it.

Use the right sander

Orbital sander

Despite the name, an orbital sander can be any shape. It's a good all round tool suitable for rough rubbing down and finishing. The orbital action may, however, leave a slightly visible pattern of scratching on some types of material. To achieve a finer finish, select a random orbit sander.

Random orbit sander

On a random orbit sander, the sanding disc is moved in orbits as on an orbital sander, but it rotates at the same time. This greatly enhances the sanding action and results in less visible marking on the finish.

TIPS

Sanding tips

1. Always wear a dust mask and if possible work in a large, open space that is well ventilated.

2. For a smooth, pattern-free finish on timber, start with a coarse-grit sandpaper and work up to a very fine-grit. It's generally not necessary to sand finer that 180-grit.

3. Remember to sand with the grain of the wood if you want a smooth finish. Sanding across the grain can leave scratches, which become even more apparent when the wood is stained.

USING A CAULKING GUN

When using cartridge tubes of product, for adhesive or filling and sealing gaps, the best way to apply these products is by using a caulking gun.

cartridge bed

metal plunger

twist metal plunger and release gears to stop flow

gears facing up to release metal plunger

pump handle

A caulking gun releases a long, smooth and even flow of adhesive or sealer where you are working. This is especially important if you are filling visible gaps or sealing around bathtubs, sinks or showers, where the sealer is in plain sight.

Smaller tubes of adhesive or sealant have to be squeezed repeatedly, which can leave a messy, uneven finish. By using a caulking gun, you can easily create a neat line and finish off by running your finger smoothly along the applied sealant.

When sealing around fittings in the bathroom, place a layer of masking tape above and below where you will apply the sealer. Once applied, remove the masking tape before the sealer dries.

CLEANING POWER TOOLS

Regularly cleaning your tools extends their life and also allows you the opportunity to ensure they remain free from rust (if they have metal parts) and apply lubricant.

A can of DIY lubricant is essential for any workshop or toolbox. It will keep your tools and accessories rust-free and is essential for applying to moving parts. It can also be used to extend the life of cutting bits.

Keep all instruction manuals for your power tools, so that you can refer back to them.

On any larger power tools where ratchets and gears are mainly responsible for certain functions, these areas need to be kept as clean as possible.

Use a paintbrush to clean out these areas on a regular basis to prevent wear and then spray with lubricant, wiping away any excess with a lint-free or cotton cloth.

Where excess dust is allowed to build up, there is increased possibility of stress and strain on these components.

Power tools are an investment and it makes sense to clean and lubricate them on a regular basis to ensure they remain in good condition.

Use a vacuum cleaner to remove dust and particles on slotted tracks, such as those on a mitre saw. A paintbrush takes care of most of the other areas.

Once clean and dust-free, apply lubricant to moving parts – wiping away any excess so as not to attract dust.

With smaller power tools such as a jigsaw, circular saw, angle grinder and other power tools with moving parts, always keep them clean and free from dust.

Dust all moving parts with a small paintbrush and spray on a light coat of lubricant.

This is particularly important with the jigsaw blade locking mechanism, as this part can easily become stiff if not kept clean.

Power tools that have a filter system or dust vents, as in the case of a sander, need to be cleaned after use. Over time these vents become clogged up and may cause the motor to overheat. With an integral filter system, this only works to filter dust if cleaned out regularly.

Today's sanders are designed to be easy to use, and this means that many use a Velcro-type sanding pad. It is essential to keep the base of the sander clean and free from dust to prevent damaging the fastening pad. Put a clean sanding pad on the base of your sander before packing away.

After just a single use your sander can become clogged with dust. After finishing your project, take five minutes to brush the sander clean before putting away.

When cleaning accessories such as blades, wear protective gloves. Spray the blade with lubricant and then use an old toothbrush to brush away debris that has built up on the blade. Use a lint-free or cotton cloth to wipe away any excess.

Protect your accessories and attachments by storing them in airtight containers, or adding a pack of desiccant to prevent moisture from causing these to rust.

TIPS AND TRICKS FOR DIY

It is worth bearing in mind these useful tricks-of-the-trade during your DIY projects.

When using a spade bit to drill holes to a pre-determined depth, wrap a strip of masking tape around the spade bit at the depth required. This will ensure that you know when to stop drilling.

You can use a jigsaw to cut a variety of materials, but it is essential to use the right jigsaw blade for the material being cut.

When performing detailed cuts in timber or board, use an 8 or 10mm wood bit to pre-drill a hole to allow for insertion of the jigsaw blade. This makes detailed cutting far easier.

Know your drill bits - To drill a hole in any material, the correct type of drill bit must be used. For basic requirements, a set of high-speed steel twist drills and some masonry bits will probably be sufficient for the average handyman. But for more sophisticated jobs /material, other bits will be required – perhaps larger, or designed for a particular material or specific purpose.

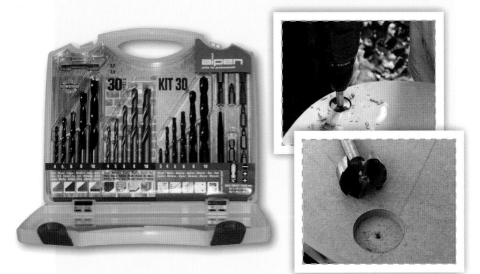

A countersink bit is used to drill out an angled depression that allows a screw head to be mounted, so as to be flush or just below the surface of your timber of board. This can then be filled in with wood filler or topped off with a screw cap to hide the screw head.

BASIC DIY: HOME MAINTENANCE

DRILLING A HOLE IN MASONRY

It is important to get this right the first time, otherwise you will end up with unwanted holes that then need to be filled in.

Masonry wall

Drill

Drilling into masonry or brick is easy if you have the right drill. Ask your local DIY store for advice. With the right drill in hand, the next item you need is a masonry bit.

Screws

Using the length of the wall plug, choose a screw that is just slightly longer.

Nylon wall plugs

Whatever you are hanging on the wall will need to be secure. Nylon wall plugs, as opposed to plastic wall plugs, are tough and will safely secure anything you hang.

TIPS

Detect

If you don't own an electronic detector, invest in one. Even one hole drilled in the wrong place could cost you a fortune to repair. These nifty tools locate metals and cables in the wall, so that you can drill safely.

You're ready to start:

1. Make sure you take the correct measurements and mark the exact spot where you need to drill.

2. Put on a pair of safety glasses.

3. Set the drill to hammer function. If your drill doesn't have a hammer function, it may be worth investing in one that does.

4. Hold the drill level. If you hold it at and angle, the hole will be at an angle as well.

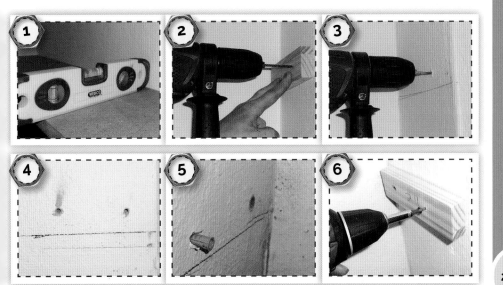

HANGING A CURTAIN TRACK

There are so many variables when it comes to putting up a curtain track or rail. It's best to measure the length of the curtains to find out how high your track will need to be.

Not all curtain tracks are created equal – rails are mounted in various ways and brackets can be anywhere.

By measuring from where the hooks will be placed you can get a fairly accurate idea of where to mount the rod without using a calculator. For example, using a tape measure to measure from where the hooks will be to the bottom of the curtain might be 220cm. Using a tape measure and pencil, you can make a mark on the wall at 220cm.

Make this mark all the way along the wall above the window, and use a spirit level to check that the curtain track will be straight once mounted. This line will be where the bottom of the track – not the brackets – will lie once mounted.

Now you need an extra pair of hands to hold the curtain track in place, with the bottom of the track lined up with your drawn mark, while you use a pencil to mark the holes in the brackets for mounting the track.

Now you can go ahead and drill the holes. Insert the correct size wall plugs. Now you can fit the track to the wall with screws.

NOTES

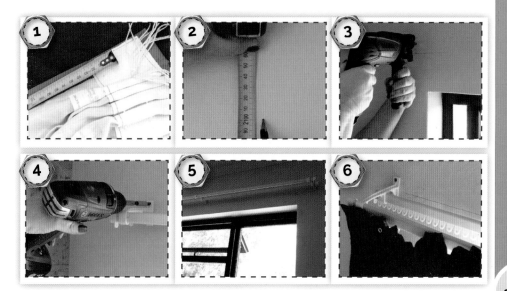

MAKING PROFESSIONAL PICTURE FRAMES

Using a biscuit joiner is most definitely the way to go if you plan to make your own picture frames. On each mitred corner use a biscuit joiner to cut the slot.

After cutting the slots it is simply a process of adding a small amount of glue inside the slots – too much glue and it will simply squish out and make a mess.

Place a fibre biscuit (you can buy these at your local DIY shop) in one of the slots and then join the two sections together to make a perfect 90-degree corner.

To hold the frame together until the glue dries, use a strap clamp (also at your local DIY store). You can adjust the strap clamp to any size and it is perfect for clamping frames.

While the frame is clamped it's easy to carry on working. You can add a back frame to allow a 5mm rebate, or lip around the back of the frame for inserting glass, mounting mats and pictures.

When having glass cut, make sure that you measure the inside dimension of the back frame. Have the glass cut about 3mm smaller than the actual dimension. To hold everything in place you can use glass clips.

The front of the frame is where you can add your detail with moulding and trim. While the frame is clamped tightly you can measure and cut moulding and trim to fit exactly.

You can add as little or as much detail as you want with pine moulding or trim, and with extruded polystyrene crown moulding.

NOTES

- - - - - - - - - - - - - - - - - - - -

- - - - - - - - - - - - - - - - - - - -

- - - - - - - - - - - - - - - - - - - -

- - - - - - - - - - - - - - - - - - - -

- - - - - - - - - - - - - - - - - - - -

- - - - - - - - - - - - - - - - - - - -

- - - - - - - - - - - - - - - - - - - -

- - - - - - - - - - - - - - - - - - - -

- - - - - - - - - - - - - - - - - - - -

- - - - - - - - - - - - - - - - - - - -

PAINTING HANDLES AND HARDWARE

When you restore or make your own furniture, you want to be able to paint handles and hardware to match the finished project.

It's not always easy to find the handles you want, and being able to paint them allows you to create handles that are perfect for your project. Painting hardware offers an inexpensive and simple way to update the look of a piece of furniture. Spray paints offer a range of colours and finishes that allow you to change the look of your handles. If you are thinking of switching your brass hardware to a pewter colour, go for either a satin or brushed nickel, or pewter finish, not a polished look. A matte finish will have a longer style life than polished, and is easier to pair up with other accessories.

Remove the existing handles or knobs and give them a good clean in warm, soapy water, or strip off any paint or varnish.

Matt or metallic paints are the best paints to use for this type of project, although gloss paint is perfect for wooden knobs.

Place the pieces out on a sheet of newspaper and spray them lightly, allowing each coat to dry before spraying on the next coat. Once painted and dry, check that you have painted all the nooks and crannies. Give them another coat if not.

You can paint almost any type of handle or knob to match a project, but bear in mind that plastic is not the best handle to paint, as the paint eventually wears off. But brass, metal or steel and most other types of handles can be painted if you use the right products. Chrome-plated are probably the easiest

handles to paint and all you have to do is make sure they are clean, give them a light sanding with 180-grit sandpaper and then spray on a coat or two in your choice of colour.

Brass handles require a little more preparation. It is important to thoroughly clean brass handles and then sand with 180-grit sandpaper before spraying. If you don't give them a good sanding all over, chances are the paint may chip off later on. Spray on the primer coat. When spraying on the colour, apply a very light first coat and allow this to dry before applying a light second coat.

The reason for applying only a light coat is that you want the paint to bond nicely with the metal surface.

REPLACING A TOILET SEAT

Over time, the screws that hold the seat can work loose and simply need to be tightened, but should they break off, you will need to replace the entire seat.

Tick list:

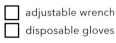

☐ adjustable wrench
☐ disposable gloves

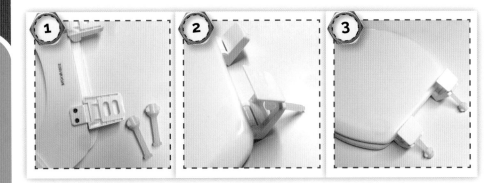

Step 1

A standard toilet seat is fitted by placing the seat on top of the toilet base. Two screws are then inserted close to the hinge, through the holes in the top of the toilet base.

Step 2

If you are re-tightening a toilet seat that has come loose, take a look underneath the toilet and locate the bolts on either side. These bolts may have a flywheel screw or a plastic screw that might have come loose and simply needs to be tightened.

Step 3

If you are replacing the toilet seat, undo these screws and lift off the seat. When unpacking your new toilet seat, note how the washers are fitted before unscrewing the assembly for fitting. Position the new seat on top of the toilet and insert the bolts into the holes, making sure that it is evenly placed on the top. Before tightening the screws, make sure that all the washers are in the right place; do not over-tighten.

INSTALLING A NEW SHOWER HEAD

Choose the shower head that meets your needs and desires. There are two main categories of shower heads to choose from: fixed or handheld. But within these categories is a wealth of options – from rain showers to multi-setting versions.

HERE'S HOW

1. Unscrew the existing shower head from the shower arm, using a crescent wrench if necessary.

2. Remove any old thread seal tape and apply new by wrapping the tape around the shower arm threads two to three times.

3. By hand, screw the new shower head onto the shower arm. Use the wrench to tighten the new shower head. If installing a handheld version, first screw the handheld bracket to the shower arm and tighten with a wrench. Then, attach the hose and handheld shower to the handheld bracket.

Now you're ready to enjoy your new shower retreat!

Fixed shower heads

Fixed shower heads are permanently mounted to the wall of the shower. Although stationary, these shower heads are far from plain. Multi-setting shower heads allow you to choose the distinct spray setting that suits your mood.

Handheld shower heads

Handheld shower heads are connected to the wall with a flexible hose, allowing a wide range of motion. Much like fixed shower heads, there are a number of handheld shower head options with finishes to add a stylish look to the bathroom.

MAKE A CHUNKY SHELF

Here's an affordable and simple way to make an attractive floating shelf. You can easily modify the dimensions to make the shelf longer or thicker. Finish it in self-adhesive vinyl, or paint it to match your decor.

Tick list:

- [ ] 2 x 12mm supawood or equivalent 200 x 500mm for top/bottoms
- [ ] 1 x12mm supawood or equivalent 100 x 500mm for front
- [ ] 2 x 12mm supawood or equivalent 36 x 200mm for sides
- [ ] 1 x 32 x 32 x 400mm pine for batten
- [ ] appropriate adhesive
- [ ] self-adhesive vinyl
- [ ] 6mm nylon wall plugs
- [ ] 55mm screws
- [ ] craft knife and cutting mat
- [ ] spirit level
- [ ] 12mm spade bit
- [ ] 5mm wood bit
- [ ] 6mm masonry bit
- [ ] electronic detector
- [ ] drill/driver and assorted bits

1. Squeeze a bead of appropriate adhesive around the edge of the front piece and gently press the top section in place.

2. Apply glue to the edges of the sides and press these in place.

3. Press the bottom section in place.

4. Make sure that all edges are flush and use a damp rag to wipe away any adhesive that has oozed out of the joints.

5. Place something heavy on top of the boards until the glue dries, or for approximately 15 minutes.

10. Remove the remaining backing to secure this to the top of the shelf, folding over the sides and removing air bubbles before folding over the top and securing to the inside of the box.

in the remaining half depth. Always use a spirit level when mounting onto a wall. Check that the horizontal bubble is between the two markers and then draw a pencil line above and below the batten.

6. Place the assembled shelf onto your vinyl and cut out around the shape. You need enough paper to cover the front, top and back, with an extra 2cm for folding inside at the back. To cover the shelf you need to cut out the covering from a single piece of self-adhesive vinyl. This will ensure that there are no loose bits that might peel open later on.

TIPS

Always use an electronic detector before drilling into walls. These handy tools tell you where power conduits and water pipes are located and will prevent expensive mishaps.

11. Finally, lift up the side flap and secure on the side pieces. Again, this can be folded over the top and secured to the inside of the box. By using a single piece of self-adhesive vinyl and securing it to the inside of the box, the vinyl won't peel off.

7. Remove the backing from the vinyl that will cover the bottom and place the shelf bottom onto this. Fold the side piece over onto the sides as shown.

8. Use your fingers to push any air bubbles to the sides and top. Then fold the vinyl over the edge and secure to the inside of the shelf.

9. Remove the backing from the section of vinyl that will cover the front of the shelf. Repeat the process described above to remove air bubbles.

12. To mount the shelf to the wall use a pine batten. The batten has two holes drilled into the front. These holes are 12mm diameter and half the depth of the batten and will allow the use of shorter screws for mounting the batten onto the wall. Use a 5mm wood bit to drill a hole

13. Place the batten against the wall between the pencil marks and use a masonry bit to mark where to drill. Remove the batten and drill 6mm holes for the nylon wall plugs. Remember to drill the holes 5mm longer than the length of the plug. A handy tip is to wrap masking tape around the drill bit as a depth guide.

14. Insert the nylon wall plugs and tap with a hammer to ensure they are flush with the surface of the wall. Insert the screws and attach the batten securely to the wall.

15. Place the shelf on the batten. To secure the shelf to the batten, add a couple of screws through the base of the shelf.

CUTTING ALUMINIUM BLINDS

Aluminium blinds are stunning, but often don't come in the right size. This is where owning a multi-tool type power device really comes in useful!

GOOD TO KNOW

It is ABSOLUTELY essential that you wear safety glasses or goggles when cutting through metal (or any other materials). Sparks will fly!

1. Measure and mark how much needs to be cut off with a permanent marker so that it is easy to see the line as you cut. Use your multi-tool device and cutting disc to remove the required amount from each side of the blind. Cut off on both sides so that the blind will look balanced once mounted.

2. Remove the plastic end caps and keep the blinds closed up tight to cut. As you cut through each side, turn the blind over to carry on cutting through. It's a good idea to clamp the blinds to a sturdy workshop table so that you can hold the multi-tool device with both hands, as the disc can sometimes slip out as you work. Cover the blinds with a towel to prevent the clamp from damaging the finish.

3. Once you have cut right through both sides of the blind, pop a grinding stone into your device, and on low speed lightly smooth the edges and remove any loose filings left behind. You can also use the grinding stone to make sure that the edges are perfectly level. Put the end caps back in and hang up your blinds.

NOTES

41

STRIPPING PAINT WITH A HOT AIR GUN

Removing layers and layers of paint takes a long time and can be extremely messy, especially if you use a sander or chemical paint stripper. It's easier with a hot air gun.

No special technique is required other than to get the hang of pointing the gun in the right direction in order to be able to manoeuvre the scraper behind the paint, to make scraping off much easier and quicker. Simply guide the nozzle over the area in a slow circular motion. Never allow the gun to point directly at one spot for more than a few seconds.

Though the heat gun does not produce a flame, the heat is hot enough to cause scorching, and in some cases, can set the wood on fire. As the paint begins to bubble, gently scrape the softened paint from the surface with a putty knife or paint scraper.

Of course, if you need to remove water-based paints you will still have to resort to using chemical strippers.

NOTES

SAFETY FIRST

A hot air gun is an easy tool for a beginner to use, but should still be handled carefully. Be constantly aware of the high temperature reached when the air gun is operating on maximum power.

Do wear thick gloves when using a hot air gun.

Due to the chemical nature of paint and plastics, work in a ventilated area to reduce any possibility of inhaling toxic fumes.

After use, have a suitable place to put down the hot air gun while it cools. The heated nozzle can melt nylon, plastic and other synthetic materials while still hot.

DEALING WITH DAMP

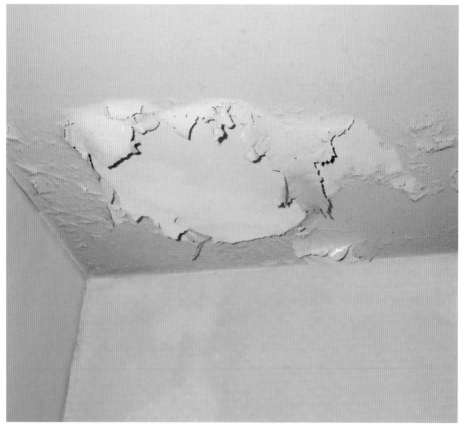

Damp can affect any home and, with the obvious health and comfort issues, it is always wise to spot any problems early and remedy them quickly. What are the causes of damp?

Although most damp problems are much less serious than they actually look, whatever the cause, damp can be very bad for our health. From aggravating respiratory problems to encouraging the emergence of mites and mould, the effects of damp can be serious, not to mention making the whole property cold and unappealing. In many cases, damp can be unwittingly encouraged due to poor maintenance. Damp can be in or around the roof, walls, floors, windows, doors or pipe-work on any property.

Rising damp

This is caused by water soaking up through porous materials into the floors and walls of the property. The obvious signs of rising damp to watch for include the walls feeling damp and cold to the touch, or the appearance of distinguishing 'tide-mark' on the inside walls. Internal decorations can become stained and damaged, and plaster can become loose.

Classic rising damp is usually worse at the bottom of a wall than at the top. The most common cause is 'bridging', when earth from the garden butts up directly on to the house wall, trapping moisture. This can be remedied by simply digging away all the soil to see if it makes a difference. If not, you may need to look into installing a damp proof course (DPC), or if you have one, it could be failing to do its job due to other factors.

In old properties, it may prove difficult to install a DPC, so a method whereby chemicals are injected into the problem areas may be the only solution.

Penetrating damp

This is caused by issues with the building or plumbing, where a problem has allowed water to enter the property. Symptoms will usually only occur during wet weather, but it can affect roofs and ceilings, along with walls. A watermark might appear, and grow if the water continues to enter. If not fixed, plaster may start to perish. Penetrating damp can be tricky to pin-point, and often may require expert help.

The first step is to check everything in and around the property.

Examine gutters, downpipes, flashing, rendering and window frames in detail. Always make sure that downpipes are unobstructed, and check if the guttering needs replacing. Check the rendering to see if it's cracked, plus look at re-sealing any gaps around window frames.

Check underneath windowsills where there should be a drip groove to shed rainwater, before it gets to the house wall. If this is blocked with moss, dirt or cement, clear it thoroughly.

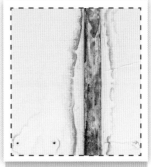

Condensation is caused by excessive moisture that cannot escape from the property. If there isn't sufficient ventilation, condensation will arise and moisture will be in the air, even if you cannot see it. Mould may appear on walls, ceilings, furniture and even curtains. There is usually a strong musty smell present.

A portable humidifier, which will suck up moisture in the air, can help, as will maintaining regular heating, and adequate insulation. To remove mildew caused by condensation, scrub well with a mix of hot water and bleach. Leave it to work for several minutes, and then clean off thoroughly.

PLASTERING WALLS

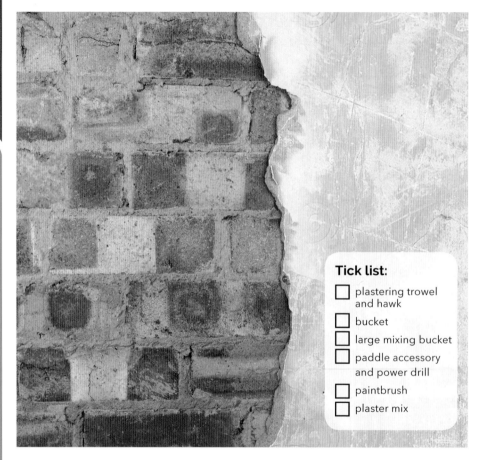

Tick list:

- [ ] plastering trowel and hawk
- [ ] bucket
- [ ] large mixing bucket
- [ ] paddle accessory and power drill
- [ ] paintbrush
- [ ] plaster mix

Plastering needs practice and a good technique for perfect results. It is possible to tackle smaller areas with good results but leave ceilings to the professionals.

This is an advanced project and you really need practice to get a good finish, but you've got to start somewhere!

1. Clear the area of furniture and spread plenty of plastic sheeting over the floor. If you are plastering over new plasterboard, press joining tape over all the board joints and screw metal reinforcing angle bead to all external corners.

2. Mix your plaster according to the instructions on the bag. Always add the plaster to the water and use a clean mixing bucket. It's essential to mix the powder and water thoroughly so that you have a thickish, creamy consistency with no lumps. A paddle accessory fitted to a corded electric drill is the best method of mixing.

3. Scrape a trowel full of plaster off the mixing board and onto your hawk. Next, transfer half the plaster to your trowel. Keep your trowel wrist straight and use your other hand to move the plaster from hawk to trowel.

4. Working from the bottom of the wall, use smooth strokes to press the plaster onto the wall. Gradually narrow the gap between the trowel's top edge and the wall as you move the tool upwards. Always keep the trowel at a slight angle to the wall at the end of the stroke. If the trowel is flattened against the surface it may pull the new plaster away from the wall.

5. Work over the whole area, aiming to apply a base coat. Don't worry about any uneven areas or holes at this stage. This coat should be around 2mm thick.

6. Level and smooth the surface. Do this when the plaster has hardened slightly but is still pliable. Use your trowel at a very shallow angle to the wall and smooth the surface. You can add a thinner skim of more plaster to fill holes and even out depressions.

7. Leave the plaster to dry once more for around 30 to 40 minutes. Now the plaster can be polished. Wet the face of your trowel and flick water onto the wall with a large paintbrush. The idea is to provide just enough lubrication for your trowel to float over the surface and fill tiny holes and imperfections. Work in regular sweeping strokes and finish with long continuous strokes across the wall.

REPAIRING DAMAGED PLASTER

Cracked, chipped or plaster that has fallen off the wall are all easy repairs to tackle yourself, and if you have acquainted yourself with basic plastering techniques, these are jobs that can be done in a weekend.

Although plastering takes a bit of practice to master the technique, you will be able to handle your own plastering projects in and around the home, saving yourself a lot of time, hassle and money!

If you're planning to do regular home maintenance projects, it's a good idea to kit yourself up with a selection of tools that will come in handy. For this project you will need to have a hawk or board, plastering trowel and a wooden float, as well as a small bag of cement and washed plaster sand.

1. Where plaster has cracked or chipped you need to prepare the area first. For plaster that has broken off completely, remove any remaining loose pieces and clean out the area with a soft brush. If you are concerned about cracks, call in a professional building contractor.

2. Mix only as much plaster as you can use in two hours. If your mix stiffens, add some water to regain workability. After two hours the unused plaster should be discarded. If there are any signs of damp on the brickwork, use a damp seal as a preventative measure before plastering.

3. Starting at the bottom, take a small amount of plaster with the plaster trowel and with a quick flicking action, apply to the wall, press and smooth upwards. Repeat this to fill up the damaged area.

4. Using a wood float, dip this into a bucket of water and then smooth the surface of the plaster until it blends with the surrounding wall.

NOTES

FITTING SKIRTING BOARDS

As a finish to the base of walls, skirting boards are more than practical, they're also decorative. In fact, skirting boards, like crown moulding, are one of those small details that can make all the difference to a room.

So often they are given very little attention but they offer architectural detail that defines the character and style of an interior.

Traditionally manufactured from timber, modern materials make DIY installation much easier. Material, style, price, and ease of installation are the four factors that you have to consider when buying replacement skirting boards for your home.

Preparation

Measure up the room before you start so that you can buy enough skirting to finish the project. Starting at one edge on the longest wall, measure the length to be cut and add 30 cm to allow for the angled ends. For aesthetic reasons, it's preferable to have long, continuous strips of board rather than cut several small pieces with visible joins. Allow extra length in case you make any mistakes along the way!

1. Use a hammer and chisel to remove the old skirting. Place the chisel at the back of the skirting and gently tap with a hammer until the chisel fits behind. Repeat this along the length until you are able to pull the existing board away from the wall. Use pliers to remove any nails left behind. Don't forget to allow for any obstructions that prevent you from installing skirting boards, such as door frames or pipes.

2. Vacuum or sweep the area so that it is free from dust and debris before installing the new skirting.

3. To join sections together at corners (inside or outside) you need to cut the ends of the board at a 45-degree angle. A good way to work out what needs to be cut and where, is to draw yourself a diagram showing all the corners that need to be cut, and this will avoid any confusion when cutting the various angles. A compound mitre saw is the easiest way to cut angles, but you can also use a mitre saw, or a jigsaw that is fitted with an adjustable plate, or a mitre box and backsaw.

NOTES

4. Apply a thick zig zag bead of adhesive to the back of the board and then hold the board at the bottom edge and angle slightly away from the wall. Press bottom edge first against the wall and then apply pressure to the entire board. By doing it this way you create suction between the adhesive and wall for better tack between the two surfaces.

5. Apply three coats of clear or tinted sealer to your new skirting boards to provide protection, or if you prefer, paint with water-based acrylic.

51

KITCHEN CABINET REPAIRS

While most modern fitted kitchens are designed to withstand constant use and abuse, an older kitchen may be taking strain. Here are some repairs you can tackle in a day.

Bottoms up

The thin board used for drawer bottoms sometimes gets wavy, or even falls out. Stiffen up the bottoms with 6mm plywood. Cut the board to fit over the drawer bottom, leaving about a 3mm gap on each side. Apply wood glue on the drawer bottom and set the board over it. Clamp in place until the glue dries.

Tighten it

If cabinet hinges are loose, or screws in your hinges turn but don't tighten and the screw hole is stripped, there is a solution. Remove hardware and apply a drop of wood glue to the ends of toothpicks and cram as many as will fit into the hole. Wipe away any excess glue. Let the glue dry, then use a craft knife to cut flush with the cabinet or drawer. Re-install the hardware, driving the screw through the filled hole.

Lubricate well

A few minutes of cleaning and lubricating can make drawer slides glide almost like new. You can remove most drawers by pulling them all the way out, then either lifting or lowering the front of the drawer until the wheels come out of the track. Wipe the tracks clean and coat them with a light spray lubricant. Also lubricate the rollers and make sure they spin easily.

Colour in

Repair scratches on kitchen cabinets with a special wax crayon from DIY stores. They come in various wood tints to match your existing finish.

Catch up

A catch that no longer keeps a door closed is either broken or out of adjustment. Catches are fastened with two screws, so replacing a damaged catch is simple. Adjustment is just as simple, but you might have to readjust the catch a couple of times before you get it right. Loosen the screws, move the catch in or out, and tighten the screws. If the door doesn't close tightly, try again.

Door hanging

If your cabinet doors are out of whack and you have European-style hinges, you're in luck. These hinges are designed for easy adjustment – all you have to do is turn a few screws. If the door isn't flush, adjust the screw depth. This screw moves the door in or out. If your hinges don't have depth screws, start with the side screws.

For a crooked door, adjust the side screw. This moves the door from side to side. In some cases, you have to loosen the depth screw slightly to adjust the side screw.

If the door is too high or too low, use the mounting screws to raise or lower the mounting plates. Loosen the screws at both hinges, slide the door up or down and tighten the screws. Some mounting plates adjust by turning a single screw.

NOTES

- - - - - - - - - - - - - - - - - -

- - - - - - - - - - - - - - - - - -

- - - - - - - - - - - - - - - - - -

- - - - - - - - - - - - - - - - - -

- - - - - - - - - - - - - - - - - -

- - - - - - - - - - - - - - - - - -

- - - - - - - - - - - - - - - - - -

- - - - - - - - - - - - - - - - - -

- - - - - - - - - - - - - - - - - -

- - - - - - - - - - - - - - - - - -

PAINTING PROJECTS

PAINTING BRICK WALLS

Face brick walls in your home can impart a sense of age and texture to a room, but they can also easily overwhelm a small space, so take care choosing the right colour and finish for your wall.

There are some people who believe exposed brick should never be painted. People on the other side of the issue feel that brick is heavy and dark and the best path to happiness is a coat of paint.

TIPS

Whitewashing

If you don't want a solid colour on the wall, but rather a lightening effect, whitewashing is the best option to choose. It is also much easier to remove if you change your mind later on. Bricks washed over with watered down matt paint rather then covered up show variation in tone and depth making it more interesting to the eye. It achieves the lighter, softer look you want yet you can still see the brick underneath.

Cover up with dropcloths before you start. Mix 50:50 paint and water and stir well. The more water you add the more translucent the final result. Use a whitewashing brush to apply the paint to a small section at a time. Remember that unsealed brick is extremely porous and will take a lot of liquid into it before it takes on a colour.

1. Ensure that brickwork is clean and in good condition. Give the wall a good brushing with a nylon scrubbing brush and follow this up by cleaning with a vacuum cleaner to clean out between any gaps.

2. After cleaning, the mortar can be repaired and all holes or cracks filled. There are various products that can be used from interior crack filler to silicone sealer for larger gaps, such as those around windows or doors.

3. Priming interior brick is necessary to ensure proper bonding between the paint and the wall. A 100 per cent acrylic universal primer is a good choice, especially where brick is chalky, as it helps to bond the paint and reduce the number of paint coats.

4. Painting interior brick will take more time and effort than an ordinary wall. Plus, you will be in close proximity to the paint and its fumes. For these reasons water based paint should be used.

5. Lay plenty of dropcloths before starting. The easiest and quickest way to apply paint to brick is with a paintbrush as it allows you to get into the nooks and crannies of rough brickwork and mortar joints. Have various sized brushes for different tasks.

NOTES

PAINTING GUTTERS

Painting gutters and downspouts is a project that adds curb appeal when combined with painting a home exterior. If galvanised gutters and downspouts are looking drab, or perhaps rusty, they can easily be refreshed.

1. Many types of gutters and downspouts are powder-coated or have a baked-on enamel finish. When this tough exterior is stained, power washing will typically not be able to remove the problem. Instead, apply a water-based degreaser. Rinse well and allow to dry.

2. Remove peeling paint with an all-purpose paint remover. For galvanised gutters, rust must be sanded back to a bright metal finish. Use a multi-sander and 120-grit sanding pads to sand back. Wash the gutters with a water-based degreaser, rinse well and allow to dry. Galvanised gutters need to be primed with a suitable primer for a high performance barrier against rust.

3. Finish your gutters with two coats of a water-based enamel for a durable long-lasting and chalk-resistant finish. If you need to paint PVC gutters, clean the surface with a water-based degreaser, rinse well and allow to dry. Then apply a water-based enamel.

VERDIGRIS FINISH

Verdigris allows you to add another element to decor accessories and fittings, such as wrought iron.

Tick list:

- [ ] acrylic craft paint – 3 shades of green + base coat
- [ ] guilding paste – copper or bronze (or metallic copper/ bronze acrylic craft paint)
- [ ] mutton cloth
- [ ] sea sponge
- [ ] paintbrush

1. Apply base coat of black or dark grey acrylic over the entire surface.

2. Pour first colour into a suitable container and dip the natural sponge lightly into the paint. Dab onto the surface randomly, remembering to turn your hand every so often so as not to have a continuously repeating pattern – cover approximately 85 per cent of the item. Allow to dry.

4. Continue for the next two colours, allowing each coat to dry before applying the next colour. Leave to dry overnight.

5. Apply a small amount of gilding paste around the edges and to highlight any relief work. Leave this to dry for an hour and then polish with a clean cloth If you are substituting with metallic craft paint, lightly sponge over the entire surface, only randomly covering the object.

3. Do not cover the entire surface; leave plenty of space for the remaining colours, and you still want to see the base coat showing through.

TIPS

When applying the metallic finish, stand back from time to time to look at the object. Transform fittings with a delicate verdigris patina to create a beautiful aged effect.

PAINTING EXTERIOR WOOD

Painted wood adds another element to a garden and home. Add colour to a garden shed or Wendy house, or paint your front door in a bold, eye-catching colour.

Tick list:

- [ ] nail punch
- [ ] hammer
- [ ] multi sander with 80- and 180-grit sanding pads
- [ ] exterior wood filler
- [ ] fast-setting polymer compound
- [ ] exterior silicone sealant
- [ ] wood primer
- [ ] acrylic paint suitable for exterior use

1. Use a hammer and nail punch to drive the heads of any nails that are standing out. These can then be filled in with exterior wood filler or fast-setting polymer compound.

2. Use a high-pressure spray to remove flaking paint, or a paint scraper or a heat gun if there are several layers of paint. Old paint must be scraped from your wood surface or your new paint will eventually flake and peel off. Make sure the surfaces are dry.

3. Sand the surfaces with 80-grit sandpaper to remove any loose paint. The surface needs to be clean before painting. Timber that has been previously oiled or sealed should be rubbed down with fine steel wool and mineral turpentine before painting.

4. Apply wood primer to the surface.

5. Once you've primed the surface, apply an exterior acrylic silicone sealant to all the seams and cracks, shaping it with a moist rag as you apply it. Let the sealant set (usually a couple of hours) before painting over it.

6. Apply two coats of suitable exterior acrylic paint directly to the timber. Allow each coat to dry completely before applying the next coat.

NOTES

SPRAY PAINT PINE FURNITURE

You can makeover any piece of furniture in your home. It's simply a matter of knowing what to do and doing it right. For example, here's how to go about giving a varnished pine chest of drawers a fresh, new look.

1. Sand the varnish

If the piece is still in good condition you will only need to give a light sanding with 180-grit sandpaper. Where there is damage you will need to sand with 120-grit sandpaper. You can use a multi sander, orbital sander or random orbital sander.

2. Repair with wood filler

Wipe the piece down with a cloth slightly dampened with mineral turpentine. This not only cleans away any dust, but also prevents the wood from sucking moisture out of the wood filler and causing it to dry too quickly. Deep dents and scratches can be filled in with wood filler. Leave it to dry and then sand smooth using 240-grit sandpaper. There's no need to apply big globs of wood filler, just enough to fill the hole and sit slightly on top of the surface. If you apply too much wood filler in one go it will crack.

3. Inspect and repair

It isn't always easy to see any uneven spots, so apply a light coat of spray paint, as this makes uneven areas very visible. If there is a low spot that requires more filler, now add this, let dry and sand smooth before painting.

4. Spit and polish

When using wet/dry sandpaper, moisten the surface and then rub with 800- or 1000-grit sandpaper. By rubbing in a circular motion you can rub away any excess for a nice smooth finish.

5. Glorious gloss

Use a protective enamel spray. Always shake the can well before use. A short burst on a scrap piece of wood will ensure that the flow is running when you spray onto the surface of your project. When applying the spray paint, hold the can at a slight angle downwards and have it no less than 30cm away from the surface. Press the trigger to start spraying before the surface – in other words spray into the air on one side, and then spray evenly from one side to the other – keeping your finger on the trigger all the time, only releasing the trigger when you are away from the surface.

Repeat this all the way over the surface as quickly as possible, so that there are no gaps between the rows. This will leave a luxurious finish that could have been professionally applied.

NOTES

PAINTING PINE PANELLING

The initial preparation may seem like a lot of work but it's definitely worth it.

1. Begin by sanding the panelling with 80-grit sandpaper to remove any existing varnish. You can use an orbit sander or elbow grease and a sanding block. Try to remove all the varnish so that this won't crack and peel later on.

2. Lightly sand the wood trim, such as skirting, door and window facings, to allow the paint to adhere to it. Once everything has been sanded, go over the walls and trim with a clean, slightly damp cloth to remove any sanding dust.

3. Apply a wood filler to any cracks and gaps where the board meets the skirtings or around doors and windows. Allow to dry thoroughly before sanding and painting. For larger gaps against doors and window frames, use a paintable silicone sealant.

4. Use a roller with a medium nap to paint the panelling. It should have a long enough nap to fill the vertical grooves in the panelling, but short enough to leave a smooth surface.

5. Prime the panelling with wood primer. Once the primer has dried, topcoat it with two coats of acrylic, allowing each coat time to dry.

TIPS

For additional protection, or in high traffic areas such as halls and corridors, apply two coats of a water-based acrylic sealer.

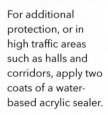

67

MAKE LIMING WAX

Finding liming wax is not easy. There are only a few select suppliers that stock liming wax, so why not make your own? You need a tin of antique wax and some white acrylic paint.

You need to mix it in well, and it helps if the wax is soft. Let it sit in a warm room for half an hour before you mix the wax and paint together.

How much paint you add is up to you. Obviously the more paint, the more intense the effect. Some experimenting on scrap wood is a good idea. Once you have mixed wax and paint together, use a soft cloth to spread this over your project.

Work in small sections, as the mix is absorbed quickly and you need to spread and rub in fast. Always work with the grain if you want a consistent finish.

If you need to tone down the whiteness, use fine steel wool and mineral turpentine – rubbing with the grain – to wipe away the excess with a rag.

This method works for anyone who wants to apply a limed effect to furniture.

NOTES

- - - - - - - - - - - - - - - - - - - -

- - - - - - - - - - - - - - - - - - - -

- - - - - - - - - - - - - - - - - - - -

- - - - - - - - - - - - - - - - - - - -

- - - - - - - - - - - - - - - - - - - -

- - - - - - - - - - - - - - - - - - - -

- - - - - - - - - - - - - - - - - - - -

- - - - - - - - - - - - - - - - - - - -

- - - - - - - - - - - - - - - - - - - -

- - - - - - - - - - - - - - - - - - - -

- - - - - - - - - - - - - - - - - - - -

- - - - - - - - - - - - - - - - - - - -

- - - - - - - - - - - - - - - - - - - -

- - - - - - - - - - - - - - - - - - - -

- - - - - - - - - - - - - - - - - - - -

- - - - - - - - - - - - - - - - - - - -

- - - - - - - - - - - - - - - - - - - -

- - - - - - - - - - - - - - - - - - - -

WINDOWS
AND DOORS

WINDOWS AND DOORS

Cracks around wooden window and door frames are common enough. You can repair cracks like these with a rubber protective coating spray, from DIY shops.

To prevent any over-spray, put masking tape above and below the area to be sprayed. Shake the can well and then shake again to be sure. Hold the can at least 30cm away from the surface and apply a light even stroke from one side to the other. Let each coat dry before applying the next coat until the area is filled or covered nicely.

You can repair and prevent leaks on a wide range of surfaces with this rubberised coating. Great for gutters, roofs, flashing, ductwork, PVC, masonry and concrete.

Wooden window frames do more than hold glass in place. They also add aesthetic appeal to both the inside and outside of a home. Like any timber product, they need regular maintenance to keep them looking good and extend their life.

Some people prefer to keep wooden window frames in their natural state and only stain or seal as required, but others prefer to paint the timber in and around the home.

Choose an exterior sealer that offers maximum protection for your exterior timber. A wide range is available. Some are moisture repellent and have a wax fraction that feeds the wood and combats fungal growth. Others offer excellent protection against ultra-violet radiation, wind, water, pollution and salt spray damage. Ask at your local DIY shop for more information.

REFRESHING A FRONT DOOR

It's time to strip off that old varnish and use sealer instead.

While varnish and sealer are similar in composition, sealer is of a much lower viscosity and is able to penetrate deep into the wood to moisturise and protect from within – rather like using moisturiser on your skin.

of the door. A heat gun is ideal for removing varnish of more than one layer. Don't have the heat gun too close or you will end up singeing the wood.

1. Use a drill/driver and screw bit to remove the door from the door frame by removing the screws in the door hinges. Place the door on a workbench in a well-ventilated area. If you plan to use a chemical stripper to remove old paint, it is best to do this outdoors or in the garage.

Then, use an all-surface stripper. Do yourself and your environment a favour by using an eco-friendly stripper. With the door off, it's important to apply exterior sealer to the bottom and top edges. This is where moisture normally has easy access to wooden doors.

NOTES

2. There are two methods for removing old paint or varnish, and you will probably have to use both if your door has panels or decorative detailing. Use a heat gun and paint scraper, preferably a plastic one so as not to scrape the surface

3. Beautifully restored and given a high-gloss shine, your new front door is ready to be screwed back into the frame. When using an exterior sealer, apply according to the instructions. Three coats are required, with a light sanding with steel wool between the first and second coats, to provide the maximum protection.

FITTING A NEW FRONT DOOR

Many homeowners put this project on the back burner thinking that a new door is too expensive and it isn't easy to fit. But once you get started you will realise that fitting is not as difficult as you originally thought.

You will find a varied selection of wood doors at your local DIY shop, and you can choose a style that best suits your home.

1. Since doors are usually a standard size and door openings aren't, chances are you will have to cut the door to fit.

Shaving off a bit here and there is easy with an electric planer. You can set the depth to remove a small amount, or increase the depth and do a couple of runs for larger quantities. If you need to cut down the width of the door, measure and mark the amount that needs to be removed and cut this off with a circular saw. A long, straight board clamped to the door acts as a guide for straight cutting.

2. Before mounting the door, apply a weather-proof varnish to the top, bottom, sides and front and back. This is the only time you will be able to reach all

the edges for maximum protection, so follow the instructions and apply as recommended. Let it dry overnight.

3. Depending on the original mountings on the door, you may need to cut out a rebate in the new door for the hinges. A rebate is simply a recess or cut out space that allows one side of the hinge to sit flush with the surface of the door.

4. To hang your new door into a frame, simply mount the hinges to the door and then measure and mark on the frame for fitting the hinges. When hanging a new door to replace an old one, use screws that are slightly larger than the old screws. This will ensure that the door hangs properly and the screws won't come loose later on.

5. With the new door in place you can now drill out for the door lock. This also depends on the type of lock you will be fitting.

NOTES

HANGING A NEW INTERIOR DOOR

Replacing a door in an existing door frame is easier and much cheaper than pulling out the trim and frame and installing a pre-hung door, because you have the old door as a template.

You can save yourself time and money by installing a new door in the existing jamb and leave the trim intact. Hanging a door is easier than you think. All you need is a hammer and chisel, clamps, a square, drill/driver and assorted drill and screw bits, and a hole saw.

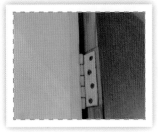

1. Measure the width of the old door. Sizes are all standard, so you'll be able to find a replacement at your local DIY shop.

2. Carefully align the top and hinge edges of both doors and clamp them together.

3. Work on a flat, level surface – or floor – to ensure that you get the correct measurements when placing the old and new door together. If the new door is longer than the old, you may need to sand or plane the top and bottom edges to fit. You can mark any difference while the doors are clamped together.

4. To cut off any excess without splintering the finish, use a guide and sharp blade in a circular saw, and deeply score the cut line

with a utility knife. Put a sharp blade in your circular saw, score the cut line and clamp on a straight edge for a guide. Set the guide so that you cut slightly to the waste side of the scored cutting line. Lightly round off the finished edges with sandpaper. If you're using a jigsaw to cut the bottom of a door, wrap a strip of masking tape about the scored line to make it easier to follow and cut a straight edge.

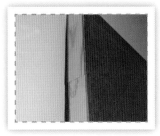

5. After making any height adjustments to the new door, clamp together once again and then use a speed square and a sharp pencil to transfer the hinge locations to the new slab. Unscrew the hinge and tape it in place to trace the rest of the hinge outline. Be sure to match the distance from the edge of the door to the edge of the hinge (the same as it was on the old door).

6. Use a hammer and wood chisel to cut out the opening for the bracket, leaving the corners for last. Use a sharp utility blade to score around the corner radius and then use the chisel to chop out the corner section.

7. Mount the hinges on the new door and hang the door. If you don't need any further adjustments, remove the door again, then finish it to match the rest of the woodwork and re-hang it.

NOTES

- - - - - - - - - - - - - - - - - - - -

- - - - - - - - - - - - - - - - - - - -

- - - - - - - - - - - - - - - - - - - -

- - - - - - - - - - - - - - - - - - - -

- - - - - - - - - - - - - - - - - - - -

- - - - - - - - - - - - - - - - - - - -

- - - - - - - - - - - - - - - - - - - -

REPLACING A WINDOW PANE

It is very easy to replace a broken window pane with the right safety gear, tools and materials.

Tick list:

- [ ] heavy gloves and goggles
- [ ] hammer and putty knife, or small chisel
- [ ] needle-nosed pliers
- [ ] primer, sealer or paint and paintbrush
- [ ] tape measure
- [ ] window putty
- [ ] replacement glass
- [ ] glazier's points or pins
- [ ] screwdriver (optional)

1. Use a hammer and putty knife or chisel to remove old putty or wooden beading that holds the old glass in place (or nails) with pliers. Remove glass. Clean out any remaining putty and dirt and brush with an old paintbrush.

3. Using a putty knife, apply putty to the channel around the opening. Position the new glass and press it firmly against the putty so it forms an even layer under the edges of the glass. For a longer-lasting and more weatherproof option, use a silicone sealant. Apply with a caulking gun according to the manufacturer's instructions.

4. On wooden window frames with beading, put a thin bead of silicone sealant around the edge of the glass. Now replace any window beading strips or glazier's points (or nails) into the frame and against the glass with a screwdriver or stiff putty knife. Use at least two a side, spaced every 100 –150mm. Scrape off excess with a putty knife.

2. Whilst you have the opportunity, paint any unfinished timber with primer and paint, or with an appropriate sealer. Have new glass cut to order by using the old glass as a pattern, or carefully measure the opening and deduct 3mm from both the length and width to allow for easy fitting.

5. Apply putty over the edges of the glass with a putty knife held at an angle and drawn firmly across the putty. Work out from the corners. The putty should not be visible from indoors. Let it cure for the recommended period of time before painting.

NOTES

FLOORS

TILING A FLOOR

This is quite straightforward, provided that you prepare carefully.

1. Find the midpoint of each wall and draw chalk lines on the floor to divide the room into quarters. The lines crossing at the centre of the room are the starting point of the tile. Space out to two rows of tiles towards the walls. If you need to cut a tile to fit against the wall it should not be less that 5cm in width. The tiles can be moved slightly to create a wider strip.

2. If you are using a pre-mixed tile adhesive you are ready to start. For powdered adhesive, mix with water until it's the consistency of mayonnaise. Mix only as much adhesive as you can use in one hour. Spread a thin layer over a 30cm square area next to the chalk line. Hold the notched trowel at a 45-degree angle to the floor and spread evenly in broad curved strokes, then finish with a straight pass, which ensures the best adhesion. Combing into furrows allows air to escape.

TIP

When spreading adhesive, press down hard so that the trowel makes a scraping sound – the trowel's notch size should equal the tile thickness.

3. Gently lay a tile on adhesive and push down with your fingers with a slight twist of the wrist. Use this same technique to set each tile. Use tile spacers to ensure even joints. Lay the next row alongside the first and continue spreading adhesive and setting tiles, working from the centre of the room out toward the walls. Every few rows, hold a framing square alongside the edge of the tiles to check that they are square to each other.

4. Make straight cuts as needed with a snap cutter. To fit a tile around an outside corner, hold one edge against the wall and mark the tile where it touches the corner. Pencil a line all the way across the tile. Then, without turning the tile, move it to the other side of the corner and again mark where tile and corner meet. Mark an X on the part to be cut away. For curved or scribed cuts you can use an angle grinder to cut out shapes and a tile nibbler for smaller cuts.

5. After the tile sets overnight, mix up a batch of grout to a runnier-than-mayonnaise consistency. Add water a little at a time by squeezing it from a sponge. Scoop some grout onto the floor with a trowel and spread it with a rubber float held at a 45-degree angle to the floor. Push grout into the joints by first moving the float in line with the joints, then diagonal to them. Work from the edges of the room toward the centre.

6. Allow the grout to set for 20 or 30 minutes. It should be firm to the touch before you begin washing the surface of the tile. Wipe away grout haze with a damp, well-squeezed sponge rinsed often in a bucket of clean water. Again, wait for grout to haze over, then wipe with clean sponge. Repeat until the tile is clean. Don't be too aggressive when wiping up grout haze, or you could pull grout out of the joints.

CUTTING CIRCLES INTO TILES

Most bathrooms require at least one hole in tiles for a floor or shower waste outlet, or for a toilet and pedestal if you are tiling an existing bathroom layout. For efficient water run-off, position the circle at the intersection of two or four tiles rather than cutting into a single tile.

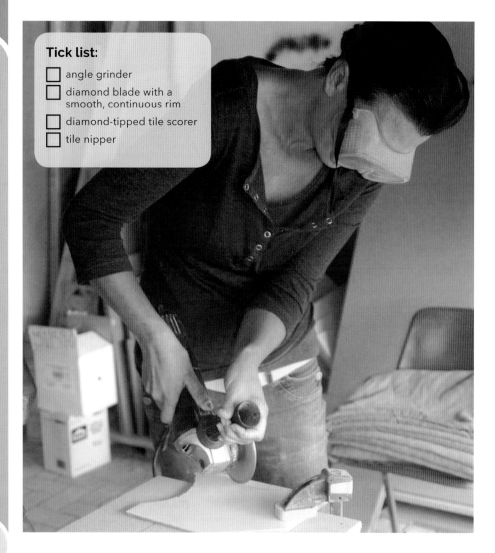

Tick list:

- [ ] angle grinder
- [ ] diamond blade with a smooth, continuous rim
- [ ] diamond-tipped tile scorer
- [ ] tile nipper

NOTES

1. Mark the circle on the tiles then score the profile with a diamond-tipped tile scorer. Follow this mark with the angle grinder, applying light, gentle pressure to the surface of the tile.

2. Before removing the excess tile, make short cuts on both sides of the semicircle. Connect the cuts by making a series of progressively deeper shallow cuts.

3. Complete the semicircle with a series of spoke-like radial cuts. Clean up rough edges with a diamond blade or remove tabs with a tile nipper.

4. Grind the edges smooth, working slowly around each curve.

LAYING A PARQUET FLOOR

Installed using small blocks or slats of wood in varying patterns and designs, parquet floors are a beautiful addition to the home.

Patterns for parquet floors may be herringbone or basket-weave, or more complex designs incorporating squares, triangles and lozenges of differing wood species. As with any wood floor, Parquet needs regular maintenance to ensure that it stays looking good.

Scratched floor

If the floor is badly scratched, you may need to hire an orbital floor sander for the day to smooth down the surface.

1. Before starting to sand, make sure that any loose blocks are removed and placed out of the way for the time being.

2. With a medium grit sanding pad (80- or 120-grit), start at the far side of the room and guide the floor sander over the area to be sanded. As you complete one strip, turn around and repeat until you have completed the entire floor.

3. Repeat this process with a 220- or 240-grit sanding pad; this step reduces the roughness left by the medium grit sandpaper and leaves a smooth surface ready for sealing.

4. Clean up all the remaining dust with a water filtration vacuum cleaner. This is by far the best option, as it doesn't re-circulate dust back into the air. Another alternative is to use a mop lightly dampened with mineral turpentine to wipe away the dust.

Stain and seal parquet flooring

You can purchase a ready-tinted sealant in various colours, or purchase a clear sealant and mix in your own stain. Whatever option you choose, you will need a quality indoor sealer that is specifically designed for wood floors.

1. Apply the sealant liberally, especially when covering a large area, and use a paintbrush for around the perimeter. If the sealant is immediately absorbed into the wood in under five minutes, apply additional sealant. Leave to dry completely.

2. Use ultra-fine steel wool to lightly rub over the sealed surface to remove excess sealant. Wipe clean once you have rubbed down.

3. Apply a second and third coat of sealant to the floor, allowing each coat to dry thoroughly. The floor will be touch-dry after 24 hours, but refrain from replacing furniture into the room for at least 2 days to ensure proper curing of the product.

To extend the finish of your new floor and keep it looking good for longer, simply wipe with a soft, dry mop regularly.

NOTES

STRIPPING STONE TILE FLOORS

If there is one project that instantly refreshes a home, it's stripping excess wax build up from natural stone tiles and applying a fresh coat of sealer.

Tick list:

- ☐ large, stiff bristle scrubbing brush or broom
- ☐ mop
- ☐ 2 large buckets
- ☐ polish remover/stripper
- ☐ rags

Over time the build up of wax on stone tiles dulls the finish and looks drab. The purpose of stripping a floor is to remove built-up layers of sealer or wax to restore it to its original state, or as close to it as possible. Most commonly, this is done in order to reseal the tiles.

1. Remove all furniture from the room. This is a great opportunity for you to take upholstered chairs outdoors and give them a good cleaning. Use wide masking tape to cover skirtings and trim, especially metals, to prevent the stripper from damaging the finish. Open doors and windows to let in fresh air and keep the space well ventilated.

2. It's better to only strip a small area at a time since it is very important that the stripper does not dry on the floor. Apply a liberal coat of stripper to the area and leave for five minutes. Bear in mind that the more wax build up, the longer it will take for the stripper to work. It may even be necessary to strip the same area twice. Be aware that the floor will be very slippery when the stripper has been applied, so avoid walking on it if possible.

3. Dip the scrubbing brush or stiff broom into a bucket of clean water, tap off excess water and start scrubbing the surface. Keep the surrounding area dry as you work. The stripper goes milky-white as the water neutralises the stripper. You will need to dip and brush a few times.

4. With a fresh bucket of water, use a mop to wash the area and then wipe clean with a damp rag. Check to ensure that the tiles are stripped clean, or repeat the process if necessary. There should be no opaque or whitish areas on the surface of the tiles. Empty out the bucket and add clean water and then move onto the next area to repeat the process until the entire floor has been stripped.

Allow the floor to dry overnight before applying a natural stone sealer in accordance with the instructions.

TIP

Do yourself a favour and use a stiff broom instead of a scrubbing brush. Far less work!

NOTES

SANDING AND SEALING A WOODEN FLOOR

1. To brighten up scuffed and scratched wooden floors, run the orbital sander across the floor. Then sand around all the edges and get in the corners.

2. The job goes much faster with a disc sander. This does an amazing, albeit slow job. Vacuum and clean the floors with mineral spirits to remove all dust and dirt particles from becoming a permanent part of the floor.

3. Staining the floor is hard work and you think it will never get done. At the end though, you can stand back and enjoy your beautiful floor and all your hard work. Use a clear floor sealer and buy a separate tint to stain in the colour that you want. Start in a far corner and then work your way backwards from that spot.

If there are any doors or walkways that are going to be used, close these off until the floor is dry. Drying time depends on the weather, but follow the instructions on the tin.

4. Regardless of the type of finish you apply, remember that there is a difference between dry time and cure time. A finish may dry in a matter of minutes, but it will not achieve its maximum hardness until it has had time to cure - typically in about seven days.

Once dry, you can walk on the floor in bare feet or socks, but keep shoes and pets off it for an another day. If possible, wait three days before bringing in rugs and furniture. Regardless of how long the finish has cured, never slide furniture across a hardwood floor, as it can leave an unsightly scratch in even the strongest finish.

WOODWORK

WOOD STAINING AND SEALING TIPS

Before you do any staining or sealing, spend time sanding down any project to achieve a silky smooth finish.

TIPS

Once you have applied stain and sealer it's too late to fix up any rough edges, unless you are prepared to start again from scratch. Use 120-grit for areas that require intensive sanding and then finish off with 240-grit sandpaper.

1. Use a cloth lightly dampened with mineral turpentine to wipe your project to remove all traces of dust. In corners and detailed areas you can use a paintbrush to brush away any stubborn dust. To stain and seal, use a low-gloss exterior sealer that will enhance the wood grain and provide protection from the elements. This is especially advised if your project, for example, a garden table, is going to be outdoors for most of the year.

2. Use a varnish paintbrush when applying sealer (or varnish), as this has stiffer bristles. It's also important to dip the brush into the sealer and not wipe off on the side of the can. Instead let excess sealer drip off the brush back into the can to prevent air bubbles being trapped.

Apply the first coat with smooth, even strokes along the grain of the wood. Any drips at the starting point will be absorbed into the cut edge or end grain and will be sucked up very quickly. You can easily wipe away any drips that aren't absorbed.

3. Start on the top or uppermost surface of any project and then work down the sides and finish the remainder. Apply sealer to the undersides as well. When applying the first coat, it should stay wet for at least 10 minutes. If the sealer is absorbed quicker than that,

By brushing with the grain from one end to the other you avoid patchy areas. If you run out of sealer before reaching an end, dip the brush and immediately continue from where you left off, blending the area together by brushing backwards and forwards along the grain.

apply more first coat until the surface stays wet. That way you know the wood has absorbed sufficient sealer.

4. Let the first coat dry thoroughly and then wipe the surface with steel wool. This allows optimum penetration for the second coat. By wiping away any excess, you allow the wood to absorb as much sealer as possible. Apply the second coat in the same way as the first and allow this to dry before applying a third and final coat.

REPAIRING SCRATCHES IN WOOD

Don't let a damaged wood table put a damper on the decor.

Tick list:

- [ ] mineral turpentine
- [ ] coarse and soft cloths
- [ ] steel wool
- [ ] antique wax
- [ ] wax crayon for wood – from DIY shops

The minor nicks, scuffs and hairline scratches that come with everyday wear and tear are one thing. Without them, an old piece looks devoid of character. But a water ring, an alcohol stain or a deep unsightly scratch is another matter. These types of blemishes can be relatively easy to repair without resorting to removing the finish.

1. Dampen a coarse cloth with mineral turpentine and gently rub the cloth over the table in the direction of the grain to soften any protective surface layer of wax. Use a clean cloth to wipe off any residue. If your table has recesses or deep moulding around the edges or along the legs, use a piece of steel wool or a soft toothbrush, dipped in mineral turpentine, to lightly wipe away wax build-up and grease in the crevices. Then clean off the surfaces again with the soft cloth and mineral turpentine.

2. Use a soft cloth with antique wax and rub the dull, cleaned finish vigorously to buff out hairline scratches or white rings and revitalise the surface until it shines. Follow the instructions on the tin for a professional finish.

3. To fix a small scratch, use a wax crayon for wood to fill in and blend the scratch. Let it dry for an hour, then buff away the excess wax colour with a soft cloth.

4. To repair deeper scratches, rub the edge of a wood-coloured wax stick that matches your table over the scratch until it is filled. Wipe off the excess and buff with a soft cloth. Use a compatible finish to fill in even deeper scratches.

5. Apply antique wax and leave to dry, then buff to a high shine. You may have to build up the polish in some areas to disguise rings or patches worn into the finish.

NOTES

FAST FIXES FOR WOOD FURNITURE

Wood furniture, especially when made from hardwoods or exotic woods, should be treasured for its value. It's important to restore and repair wood furniture whenever possible.

Chipped corners

Damage happens, but luckily there are now products that can easily fix it. If you have dents or pieces chipped off, you can use wood putty. It offers a quick and easy way to repair wood and can be moulded like clay to repair, rebuild, or restore anything made of wood. Once you have moulded and smoothed the putty into place, leave it for about an hour before sanding, then stain it or paint it to match the rest of the piece.

You can add colour to wood putty by adding a small amount of oil paint to the mix. Combine colours until you achieve an exact tint to match the existing piece.

Dented furniture legs

You can use wood putty to repair dents in wooden legs on tables and chairs. Use it to restore the shape of wood carvings and wood parts such as handles or knobs, or to replace dry rot, insect damage and worn wood.

Wobbly legs

Even modern furniture needs attention from time to time. Table legs fastened with screw brackets can become loose and legs wobbly. It's easy to tighten a loose nut and bolt by adding a drop or two of a liquid threadlocker before re-tightening nuts. This will ensure that fastenings stay tight for longer.

Split wood

Where the wood has split, wedge open with a scrap of wood or large screwdriver and then apply wood glue to split sections using a small brush. Clamp the joint using padded clamps and be sure to remove excess glue, using a damp cloth first.

NOTES

Replace damaged veneer

Veneer is a thin (roughly 3mm) layer of pressed wood that is normally applied over a cheaper wood. Damaged veneer can be replaced; you will find a selection of veneers at most timber merchants. Where veneer has buckled and split you should be able to prise it off with a chisel. Before you put down new veneer, make any necessary repairs and sand smooth.

Apply a generous layer of wood glue to the substrate and apply a heavy weight over the surface to ensure the veneer stays flat while the glue dries.

Chewed furniture

This is a common problem for people with new puppies. Sand the chewed area to smooth before applying wood filler for small defects, or wood putty (for big defects or missing chunks – depending upon how hungry the puppy was!) Let the filler dry completely before sanding smooth with 240-grit sandpaper. Choose the tint of wood filler that most closely resembles the finished colour of the wood.

TIPS

Touch ups

Gel stain is great for covering up scratches in wood furniture. The product comes in a variety of wood tints and can be applied with a cotton bud or small cloth. On a varnished piece, use clear nail polish to cover up the damaged area. Sand with 400- or 1200-grit sandpaper to match the existing sheen.

Buff up the shine

If the varnish finish is scuffed but you don't want to strip down the entire piece, apply antique wax to restore the shine. Apply only a thin layer to the surface and use a soft cloth to wipe it around as evenly as possible. Wait 30 minutes for the product to dry and then buff it up for a nice sheen.

DEALING WITH WOODWORM

Woodworm can cause extensive damage to your home and furniture if left untreated. When wood is moist it creates the perfect environment for fungal and microbial attack, and the ideal home for woodworm, which can reduce wood to hollowed-out beams in no time.

In most timber used for construction, conditions are not usually ideal and any infestation will slowly die out. On the other hand, just a small amount of moisture and woodworm will thrive.

In older homes, that means particular care is required under poorly ventilated floors, bathrooms, laundry and similar environments where timber is installed.

Timber quickly absorbs moisture vapour from air. It doesn't need to be physically splashed with water to become moist.

Inspecting for woodworm

The best place to looks for the telltale small holes is underneath the floor, but if that's not very accessible, try looking around the edges, especially under windows. The entire roof should be checked, but for starters try the ceiling joists and the spars next to the chimney.

On timber staircases, look at the edges of the treads in particular. Do look carefully at the stair strings and joinery as well.

Treating woodworm

Is the woodworm active? You may get fresh holes during the summer months. New holes are usually part filled with frass which is the excretion by woodworm of undigested wood. A trained specialist can identify the species of the infestation just from the texture, size and colour of the pellets.

couple of times to ensure complete eradication of any infestation.

• For extensive damage it's a good idea to pour wood glue down the holes and then top this off with a plug of wood filler in a matching shade. Thereafter, you should seal the wood with a quality sealer.

NOTES

If you suspect an infestation of woodworm call in a specialist contractor who has experience in this field. Modern treatments include a variety of chemicals including a permethrin-based insecticide. Permethrin is a synthetic pyrethroid with very low mammalian toxicity (cats excepted). It kills woodworm stone cold, though.

Boron products work well too. A good timber infestation surveyor will make a judgement on the most appropriate product.

Woodworm and furniture

When buying wood furniture – or if you own vintage wood – check for tiny holes about 1-2mm in diameter – the first indication of woodworm. These small holes are exit holes that an adult beetle uses. If the piece is an antique, it is best to let an antique restorer attend to the problem. However, if you cannot afford to send it in to an antique restorer there are some tried and trusted methods you can try:

• Turn the piece upside down and flushing mineral turpentine fluid into all visible holes. As it drains into the tunnels, add more mineral turpentine. You will also need to treat around glued sections, such as underneath the frame, as these are often made from softwood and particularly susceptible to attack, as well as the bottom of legs or feet, which are ideal spots for eggs to be laid.

• Place the piece outdoors and allow to dry thoroughly before using it. Repeat this process a

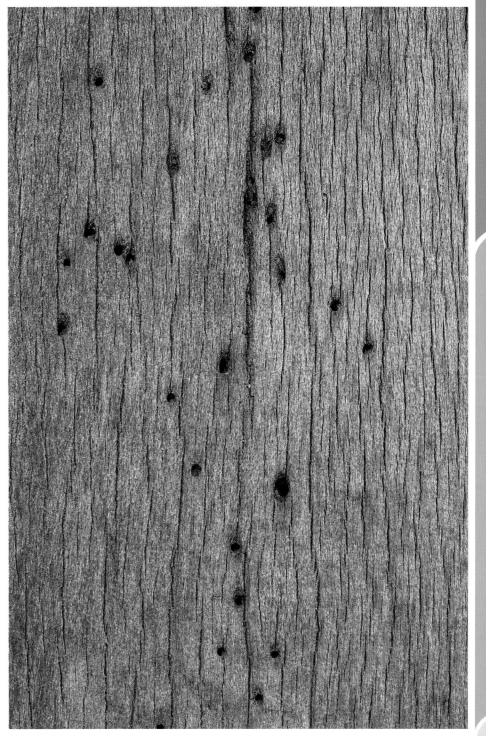

GETTING THE AGED WOOD LOOK

Even if you cannot find reclaimed timber, it is possible to create the aged wood look yourself.

You can make ordinary laminated pine shelving look like reclaimed timber furniture. The trick is to use wood gel stain and some common household products to age new timber and make it look authentic.

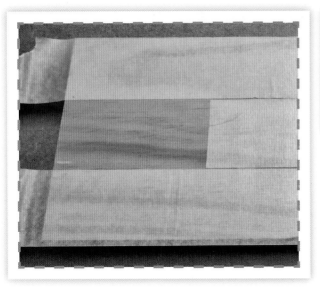

1. Use wide masking tape to mask off blocks, as you would normally see on most reclaimed timber furniture.

4. As the final treatment, and the one that really adds the most ageing effect, soak steel wool for a couple of days in vinegar. It smells awful but works like a dream. Use a paintbrush to spread the rusty vinegar solution over the wood and then squeeze out the steel wool and rub over once or twice to get some of the muck into the gouges and dents.

3. There are a few things you can do to complete the authentic reclaimed timber or aged wood effect. To distress new wood, use a hammer, some lengths of chain and assorted screws to scrape the wood to create panels or strips. Let your inhibitions go and experiment with what you have.

2. You can use a wood gel stain or household items such as wet teabags, brown vinegar, or balsamic vinegar for a darker effect. Soak a steel wool pad in vinegar for a couple of days before you start. Remove and replace the masking tape as you apply the various treatments to individual sections.

REPAIRING WOOD FURNITURE

Being able to repair and restore wood furniture means that you can extend the life of the beautiful pieces you already own, and even consider buying a piece of wood furniture that is in need of some care and attention.

Solid wood furniture has become extremely expensive and being able to pick up a bargain is the only way some of us can own furniture that is built to last a lifetime or two.

An item such as this old bench just needs a bit of time spent on it to transform it into a lovely piece of furniture. Follow the steps below to see how.

1. Sand to remove all the paint splotches and spatters. This piece has a large chip missing at the edge. Also the surface of the wood has cracked in places where it has dried out. It's important to remember that wood requires constant nourishment to keep it looking beautiful. Regular application of a protective oil or seal penetrates deep into the wood to protect it. Without regular application, the wood starts to shrink as it dries out.

2. The easiest way to fix dents and dings, or repair missing chunks, is to use wood putty. This is kneaded together and then applied to the lightly sanded surface to be repaired. Once kneaded, apply the resin forcefully onto the surface and push down and out with your thumb over the surface to ensure a good bond with the wood. If you don't do this, there is a chance that the product will simply fall off when you start sanding.

3. Smooth the resin before it dries, as the product becomes rock hard once cured and difficult to sand. Have a small bowl of water handy, so that you can wet a finger to smooth down the resin. Use the tip of a finger to press down and smooth so that the resin fits and matches the surrounding levels of wood as much as possible.

NOTES

- - - - - - - - - - - - - - - - - -

- - - - - - - - - - - - - - - - - -

- - - - - - - - - - - - - - - - - -

- - - - - - - - - - - - - - - - - -

- - - - - - - - - - - - - - - - - -

- - - - - - - - - - - - - - - - - -

- - - - - - - - - - - - - - - - - -

- - - - - - - - - - - - - - - - - -

- - - - - - - - - - - - - - - - - -

- - - - - - - - - - - - - - - - - -

- - - - - - - - - - - - - - - - - -

- - - - - - - - - - - - - - - - - -

- - - - - - - - - - - - - - - - - -

- - - - - - - - - - - - - - - - - -

- - - - - - - - - - - - - - - - - -

- - - - - - - - - - - - - - - - - -

6. Now it's time to sand. Always start with a lower grit sanding pad. Use 60/80-grit for removing varnish or paint and 120-grit for all other surfaces.

a soft cloth. Work on a small area at a time, as the gel stain dries quickly. If you find that there are streaks, apply a dab of gel stain to the area to rub out.

4. Let the resin cure for about an hour, or until it is hard to the touch, but for no more than two hours. This is the best time to sand smooth, before it has the chance to cure completely and becomes extremely hard. Start off by sanding with 120-grit sandpaper and finish with 240-grit to smooth. Sand away as much of the resin as possible, leaving only that needed to fill the gap or dent. This is because resin doesn't accept a stain and will be very obvious.

7. After sanding, you'll probably notice that there are still some dark and medium patches here and there. You don't want to sand down to raw wood, as this would spoil the aged effect that the piece has acquired. Rather than start from scratch leave these patches to add to the look.

Because some of the old stain has been sanded away, use gel stain to put back some colour.

9. Apply gel stain over the entire project, so that you don't have any areas that are lighter or darker than the rest. Now you can see how the dark stain left behind shows through and give the finish an aged or vintage look.

5. Smaller cracks and dents can be filled with wood filler. This comes in a variety of wood tints and you should choose a pine if you are not staining, or a darker colour for wood to be stained. Only apply enough filler to cover the damaged area.

8. It's a good idea to stain the wood a lighter shade, as this will still allow the aged effect to show through. Put on some disposable gloves and apply the gel stain with

10. To finish off, use antique wax, sealer or varnish. Sealer and varnish are best if you plan to repair or restore a coffee or side table, or any furniture that could be damaged by water marks. However, antique wax also protects from spills and it imparts a satiny-smooth finish to the furniture.

NOTES

OUTDOOR PROJECTS

MAKE A FOLDING TABLE

Entertain in style with this lovely garden table.

Tick list:

- [ ] 6 x 140 x 1200mm pine table planks
- [ ] 2 x 44 x 1160mm pine apron, long sides
- [ ] 2 x 44 x 800mm pine apron, short sides
- [ ] 3 x 140 x 800mm pine top supports
- [ ] 4 x 44 x 44 x 730mm pine legs
- [ ] 2 x 44 x 610mm pine narrow side, cross beams
- [ ] 2 x 44 x 720mm pine wide side, cross beams
- [ ] 4 steel angle brackets, small
- [ ] 4 drop-down/flap hinges
- [ ] 16mm wood screws
- [ ] 4.5 x 65mm wood screws
- [ ] 3.5 x 3.5mm wood screws
- [ ] exterior wood sealer and stain

Tools:

- [ ] drill/driver plus assorted bits
- [ ] countersink bit
- [ ] tape measure and pencil
- [ ] carpenter's square
- [ ] jigsaw and clean-cut blade
- [ ] paintbrush

1. Sand smooth any rough edges before assembly. Always apply wood glue to joints.

2. Cut the wavy planks: On each of the planks for the top draw a wavy line and then cut out with a jigsaw. It's easiest to cut one and use this as a template to cut out the rest of the planks. Sand the cut edges smooth with 180-grit sandpaper.

3. Apply stain and sealer to the planks before assembling.

4. While waiting for the sealer to dry, you can start to assemble the top frame. To do this, attach the short sides to the long sides with steel angle braces and 16mm screws.

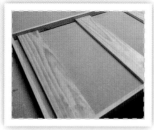

5. Working on a flat, level surface, place the top supports within the frame; one at the ends and one in the centre. Leave 20mm gaps between the support frame and the apron.

6. Pre-drill a 3mm pilot hole on the outside of the frame; countersink before attaching the frame to the top supports with 4.5 x 65mm screws.

NOTES

- -
- -
- -
- -
- -
- -
- -
- -
- -
- -
- -
- -
- -
- -
- -
- -

7. Place the assembled frame on top of the wavy planks. Make sure you leave an equal spacing all the way around. Use 3mm scraps as spacers to hold the top planks apart.

8. Use 3.5 x 35mm screws through the top supports to hold the top planks in place. Make sure you drive a screw all the way along the length and width to firmly secure the top to the supports. Drive a screw through each and every section along the top supports. Shown before, you can see that quite a lot of screws were used, but this ensures a firm table.

9. Measure down and mark at 200mm from the top of each leg. Drill 3mm pilot holes, countersink and drive 4.5 x 65mm wood screws through until the tip of the screw shows. Press a cross beam onto the screw tips to make a mark. On the mark at the end of each cross beam, drill a 3mm pilot hole. Drive 4.5 x 65mm screws through the legs and into the cross beams. One set of legs is narrower than the other, to allow the table to be folded and put away when not in use.

10. Place each set of legs flush against the inside of the apron. Attach the drop-down/flap hinges as shown. To provide protection from the elements, it is essential to apply a sealer to the table. Wipe clean to remove all traces of dust before applying three coats of exterior sealer.

TIPS

Corner clamps come in very handy when you are working on your own. It's like having an extra pair of hands to help you.

NOTES

HOW TO MIX CONCRETE

There are various different concrete mixes and each is used for a specific job. Here is an easy guide to the various mixes and their uses.

Guidelines

Use only sufficient water for a workable mix, as too much water will result in reduced strength. Mixes should be used within a maximum of two hours after being prepared and you should never add additional water.

After completing a project, it is essential to protect the concrete from the sun and wind by covering with a plastic sheet, damp sand or hessian. Spray a light misting of water over the surface daily, for at least a week, especially during hot weather.

Low strength

concrete is used for standard foundations that do not require reinforcement, such as free-standing walls.

Medium strength

concrete is used for reinforced foundations, concrete slabs, interior floors, patios, paths and driveways.

High strength

concrete is used for structural beams and slabs, pre-cast items and heavy-duty floors.

REPAIRING CRACKS IN CONCRETE

Cracks in concrete happen all the time as a result of shrinkage or movement. As concrete cures and dries out it has a tendency to shrink, and that's why it is important to lightly spray concrete with water during the curing or drying process. Another reason why concrete can crack is incorrect preparation of the mix, which is why it is essential to know the right ratios of sand, stone and cement.

Using too much water when mixing concrete can cause excessive cracking and is the single most common cause of cracks in concrete. The evaporation of excess water causes the shrinkage and reduces strength. The runnier the mix, the more shrinkage will occur. It is essential to follow the manufacturer's recommendations for mixing concrete for specific projects.

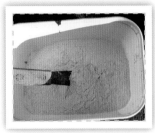

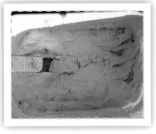

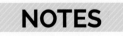

TIPS

Always clean out cracks with a vacuum cleaner before applying filler.

NOTES

After laying concrete, it is also important to prevent the concrete from drying too rapidly by either lightly spraying water on the surface, or by covering the concrete with a plastic sheet to retain moisture during the drying time.

Larger areas of concrete require what is called control joints, or cut lines in the concrete that create a weak area and force any cracks to this point. To reduce the risk of cracks, wire mesh embedded in the concrete will add strength and reinforce the installation.

Any cracks in concrete should be repaired as soon as possible, to prevent additional cracking and eventual failure of the slab. For smaller, hairline cracks you can use a hammer and chisel to enlarge the crack in a 'V' shape. The shape allows you to insert cement-based filler. This is recommended for patching floors where rapid setting is required.

Repaired concrete floors are ready for normal use (vehicular and foot traffic) after one hour. When fully cured, the applied product has a greater compression strength than conventional concrete.

Mix cement-based filler to a thick paste following instruction on the packet and apply with a putty knife or paint scraper, pushing down into the 'V' shaped gap. For longer, larger cracks it recommended that you use an angle grinder and masonry disc to cut out a 'V' shaped opening along the length of the crack.

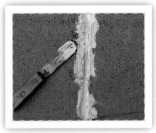

After application, use a wood float to smooth-finish the surface, or wait until the product has cured and sand smooth with 120-grit sandpaper.

REPLACING A ROOF TILE

Don't wait for missing or broken tiles to become a serious problem. Missing or broken roof tiles allow water to penetrate the roof space and wind to lift more of the neighbouring tiles. If you attend to the problem immediately you won't end up with serious repairs later on.

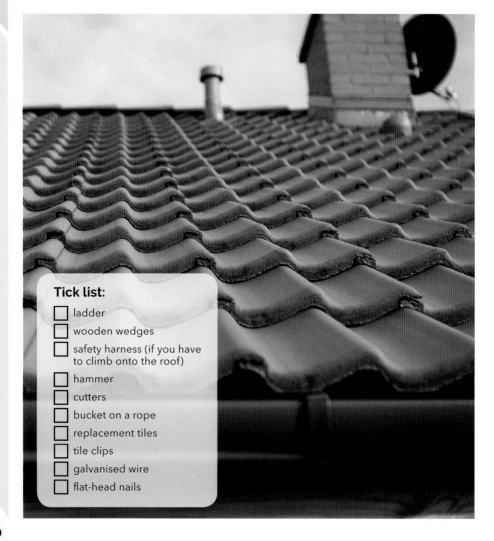

Tick list:

- [ ] ladder
- [ ] wooden wedges
- [ ] safety harness (if you have to climb onto the roof)
- [ ] hammer
- [ ] cutters
- [ ] bucket on a rope
- [ ] replacement tiles
- [ ] tile clips
- [ ] galvanised wire
- [ ] flat-head nails

1. Safety first! Secure the ladder firmly on its feet and wedge it firmly against the edge of the roof.

2. With one hand, slide up the row of tiles immediately above that overlaps the one that is to be replaced. Use the handle of a hammer or a couple of small wooden wedges to support the tiles while you work. To remove the broken tile, tilt it sideways to separate it from the interlocking tiles. You should be able to free it without disturbing them.

3. Lever the tile upwards to release it from any clip that holds it to the batten. If the tile is wired to the batten beneath (every second course is) try reaching in under the tile above with cutters to snip the ties. Otherwise, you will need to enter the roof space to free the tile. Take particular care as old tiles become very brittle with age and are easily damaged.

4. Safety first! To keep your hands free, lower the broken tile in a bucket on a rope to a helper on the ground.

5. Carefully brush dust and dirt from the grooves on the tiles either side of the space where the damaged tile was located. Be thorough, as it is these grooves that prevent water entering the roof space.

6. To fit the replacement tile, insert it at an angle, slide it into position and make sure it engages with those on either side and is firmly locked in. Lower the layer of tiles above until they are back in place, and remove your wedges.

NOTES

- - - - - - - - - - - - - - - - - - - -

- - - - - - - - - - - - - - - - - - - -

- - - - - - - - - - - - - - - - - - - -

- - - - - - - - - - - - - - - - - - - -

Replacing a group of tiles

Slide up the tiles in the row above as you would for a single tile. Tilt the lower tiles to free them. Remove the clips wherever you can. When replacing the tiles, fit the lowest course first and work from right to left. Fit a clip for each tile wherever you are able to nail it to the batten.

Lodge the hook of the clip over the ridge at the side of the tile. Hammer the nail through the hole in the clip into the top edge of the batten (near the bottom edge of the tile you are fitting).

The highest course cannot be nailed and the last tile of all cannot be fitted with a clip because the batten will be covered.

FIXING A LEAKY ROOF

If you notice water stains on the ceiling, cornice or down the walls, it's time to take a look at the roof.

Regular inspection of a roof can prevent costly repairs later on. Here are some of the things to bear in mind before attempting to repair your roof as a DIY project.

1. Use the access panel to get into the attic or roof space to inspect from underneath. Look for areas where sunlight is coming through tiles to locate a slipped or broken tile. Major leaks caused by multiple broken tiles, loose ridge caps or corroded flashings are best left to the professionals.

2. Most minor roof leaks are caused by a tile that has come loose or slipped. This is fairly easy to repair. A bad storm, especially with high winds, can sometimes cause a tile to slip out of position. Use a piece of stiff wire (or a wire coat hanger) and bend to create a hook at the end. Use the hook to pull the tile back into position along the laths (timber cross beams that support the tiles). If more than one tile has slipped, use wooden battens to lift the two overlapping tiles immediately above the tile or tiles you need to move.

3. To replace a cracked or broken tile again, use wooden battens to lift the two overlapping tiles above the cracked one. Try to pull out the damaged tile through the gap created. You may need to jiggle it from side to side if the tile has been nailed into position. As a final resort, wear gloves and goggles and break the tile to remove it. Position the new tile by manoeuvring it into place and making sure that it is bedded on the support laths.

4. Age, bad weather and poor installation can often result in leaks around skylights and other installed fittings that are attached to the roof. When you suspect a leak in this area, apply a waterproofing product and a protective membrane around the fitting.

Do I have a leak?

If there are brown stains on the ceiling, you definitely have a leak. Find the source of the problem as soon as possible. Likely culprits are a leaky roof or an overflow pipe.

Mould on the ceiling is not always an indication of a leaky roof. Ceiling mould can also be caused by damp, especially in a bathroom or laundry room. However, it is better to be safe and take a look in the attic or roof space.

NOTES

BUILD YOUR OWN DOG KENNEL

If you have a dog that is kept outdoors during the day, a good dog kennel is essential for keeping them dry in rainy weather, warm in winter, and cool in the summer months. Our dog kennel does all this – and looks good too!

Tick list:

- [ ] 1 x 648 x 800mm laminated pine
- [ ] 4 x 110 x 600mm 34mm par pine
- [ ] 2 x 76 x 580mm 20mm par pine
- [ ] 4 x 76 x 560mm 20mm par pine
- [ ] 4 x 76mm cut to length 20mm par pine
- [ ] 4 x 76mm x 600mm 20mm par pine
- [ ] 4 x 76mm x 900mm 20mm par pine
- [ ] 4 x packs of pine tongue & groove
- [ ] 4 x steel angle braces
- [ ] Wire nails
- [ ] Wood glue
- [ ] Galvanised tin for ridge cap
- [ ] Wood stain

1. Cut all the pieces to size using a jigsaw, or circular saw. On all four corners of the base [A] you will need to cut out a section to allow for the corner posts [B]. Use the corner post as a template to mark out the areas to be removed.

2. Support the base [A] on a couple of battens and cut out the rectangular sections with the jigsaw or circular saw. Use a pocket hole jig to drill recessed holes on each corner of the base [A].

3. Measure up 30mm on each corner post [B] and draw a line across. This will be the 'feet' for the kennel. Place the corner post [B] in the rectangular corner, making sure that the mark line is visible. Use smooth screws to attach the leg to the base [A]. Repeat for each corner.

4. Using the pocket hole jig, attach the front cross beams [D] to the corner post [B], making sure that the beam is flush with the front of the corner post [B]. Repeat this process to attach the side cross beams [C] to the corner post [B].

5. Dry fit tongue and groove panels to both sides. You may need to cut at one end so that the panels fit nicely onto the side frames. Starting at one side, screw all tongue and groove boards to the frame at the top and bottom.

6. Use a pocket hole jig to drill holes into the front base beam and add two upright supports [E] and screw these into place.

7. Assemble the front and sides with tongue and groove panels, using a jigsaw to cut out an opening in the front section.

8. Assemble the roof frame by joining the two front 45-degree cut sections [F] and then attaching the top and side beams [G]. Reinforce the mitred front and back sections with steel angle braces screwed to the back.

9. Attach the tongue and groove panels to the roof

in the same way as you did for the sides. Allow a 5mm overhang and the front. For the front and back of the roof section, individually cut the tongue and groove panels with a mitre saw and screw the end of each panel onto the front frame.

10. You can add pine moulding around the edge of the front section, for decoration. Use an exterior sealer to fill in any gaps.

11. Apply wood stain to the kennel inside and out. To make the roof waterproof, cut a strip of tin as a ridge cap. Fasten the ridge cap on to the top of the kennel with short panel pins. On the inside of the roof, staple thick, black plastic to the underside for extra waterproofing.

TIPS

This kennel is sized for a small to medium sized dog. You will need to increase the overall dimensions for a larger dog.

TREATING RUST

Prime and paint all iron and steel fittings in and around a home. Unpainted iron and steel will rust and deteriorate. Add salt to the equation and rust will attack unpainted iron even faster. So how do you prevent or repair rust on furniture and fittings?

Anyone living on the coast will tell you that rust attacks almost any item constructed or made from steel and iron. While this is true in many cases, rust only occurs on metals that contain iron such as unpainted or untreated wrought iron, or gates.

There is a lot of confusion when aluminium is said to rust. Aluminium does not contain any iron and therefore cannot rust, but it does corrode. Aluminium corrosion is a condition where the surface becomes dull and is sometimes crusted with calcium, lime, tarnish, or hard water stains. Where corrosion does occur, there are ways to remove it, although this differs from rust treatments.

Rust prevention

Use an appropriate primer for all mild steel and galvanised iron surfaces. Simply apply to metal fittings and furniture to prevent rust from forming. A primer offers protection against metal corrosion and degradation on all mild steel and galvanised iron surfaces.

Treating rust

When rust appears on metal or steel, immediate attention is required to prevent further damage. If left untreated, the process of rusting forms acids that eat away more layers of protection and further weakening the structure of metal or steel. Use a rust converter and primer – this reacts chemically with rust and effectively stops further corrosion. You can use a rust converter/primer for both interior and exterior use.

Where rust has eaten away the surface of metal you can use a specialised product to repair the damage – ask at your local DIY shop.

NOTES